Turquoise Unearthed

AN ILLUSTRATED GUIDE

Turquoise Unearthed

AN ILLUSTRATED GUIDE

Joe Dan Lowry
Joe P. Lowry

Rio Nuevo Publishers
Tucson, Arizona

DEDICATION

This book is lovingly dedicated to the memory of J.C. "Zack" Zachary, Jr., whose gracious spirit and sense of humor enriched the lives of so many friends and family members during his lifetime. He would often say, "Each person who has something to sell also has a story to tell." Zack cut his first turquoise stones at the age of nine, and his passion for the business continued until the day he died, November 26, 1999. He and his wife, Lillian, traveled the world, and especially throughout the American Southwest, mining and trading turquoise. This book showcases some of the finest examples from their unrivaled collection of stones and jewelry, which are exhibited to the public at the Turquoise Museum in Albuquerque, New Mexico.

ACKNOWLEDGEMENT

We are grateful to Robert Alan Zachary, lapidary and Indian jewelry trade supplier, who has spent a lifetime studying the mineralogy and history of turquoise. He also has devoted countless hours sharing his knowledge with adults and children alike.

About the authors: *Joe Dan Lowry and Joe P. Lowry operate the Turquoise Museum and are recognized worldwide for their expertise.*

Rio Nuevo Publishers®
P.O. Box 5250
Tucson, Arizona 85703-0250
(520) 623-9558, www.rionuevo.com

Text © 2002 by Joe Dan Lowry and Joe P. Lowry
Photographs © 2002 by Mark Nohl
   except as otherwise credited on page 73.

Library of Congress Cataloging-in-Publication Data
Lowry, Joe Dan, 1968-
Turquoise unearthed: an illustrated guide / Joe Dan Lowry and
   Joe P. Lowry ; photography by Mark Nohl.
      p. cm.
ISBN-10: 1-887896-33-3 ; ISBN-13: 978-1-887896-33-7
1. Turquoise—Southwestern States. I. Lowry, Joe P., 1943- II. Title
TS755.T8 L69 2002
553.8'7—dc21   2002011482

Editors: Ronald J. Foreman and Sarah Trotta
Design: William Benoit, Simpson & Convent

Front cover: Number 8 turquoise and silver bracelet
Back cover: Blue Gem turquoise and silver necklace
Title page: Blue Gem turquoise nugget
Table of Contents: Zuni jeweler with pump drill, ca. 1920

Printed in Korea   10 9 8 7 6

CONTENTS

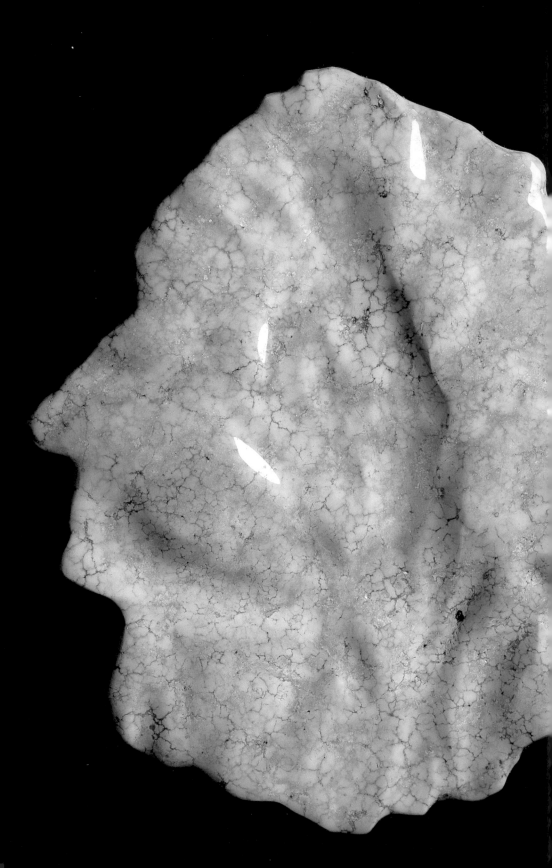

TURQUOISE: THE SKY STONE

From geologists to jewelers, miners to healers, ancient cultures to modern collectors, people the world over have long been captivated by turquoise. To the native peoples of the American Southwest in particular, this "sky stone" is an ancient talisman for health and happiness, and for centuries it has been incorporated into both ceremonial and everyday jewelry, sculpture, and pottery. Other cultures believe turquoise, one of the loveliest of gemstones, possesses protective powers.

In our modern world, where so many objects are mass-produced, turquoise appeals to us because every stone is unique. We Americans especially value the fact that turquoise comes in so many colors and varieties. In a sense, this gemstone reflects the complexity and diversity of our American culture, as well as our respect for the individual. Over time, turquoise and the wearer will form a unique bond as the body oils of the former influence the color and character of the latter.

Today, nearly all of the world's supply of turquoise to the consumer is marketed through the United States. The American Southwest, in particular, is a region uniquely blessed with some of the finest and most abundant deposits of turquoise. Here, the spiritual values, aesthetic sensibilities, and artistry of native peoples have combined with modern mining and marketing methods and a thriving tourist trade to make this gemstone a widely recognized cultural icon.

"George Washington," a 6,800-carat nugget from Turquoise Mountain, bears an uncanny resemblance to the profile of its namesake and reflects the values of individuality and diversity that make turquoise "America's Gemstone."

WHAT IS TURQUOISE?

Our common name for turquoise originated not in the United States but rather in medieval Europe, where traders from Turkey introduced the blue-green gemstones as an exotic luxury. Although this turquoise was actually obtained from mines in Persia (now Iran) medieval Europeans associated the stones with the Turkish traders who supplied them rather than the land of their origin, and so they called them "turceis" or, in later French, *"turquois."* English speakers adopted the latter French word, adding an "e" ("turquoise"), while Spanish speakers called the stone "turquesa." Here in the Western Hemisphere, turquoise was widely known for centuries by its Nahuatl name, *chalchihuitl* (pronounced chal-che-we'-tl), a term used by the Navajo and other peoples of the American Southwest until the late 1800s.

Persian turquoise

Scientifically speaking, turquoise is classified as a semiprecious, opaque mineral composed of hydrated copper and aluminum phosphate. Turquoise has a triclinic crystalline structure, and the chemical formula is $Cu(Al_6Fe)(PO_4)4(OH)8(4H_2O)$. *Dana's Manual of Mineralogy* describes turquoise as a secondary mineral derived from original, primary copper deposits that usually consist of chalcopyrite (a common yellow, metallic mineral made up of sulfur, iron, and copper) and pyrite, which resembles chalcopyrite but contains only sulfur and iron. Primary ore deposits are formed from high-temperature, metal-rich fluids.

The relative value of a particular turquoise specimen is based on its density, color, matrix, and rarity. Turquoise can range from a low-grade 5 to a gemstone-grade 7 on the geometric Mohs (rhymes with *nose*) scale used by geologists. (The hardest naturally occurring stone, the diamond, rates a 10 on the Mohs scale.) Low-grade turquoise, which is more common, is soft and porous so it easily absorbs creams and body oils and tends to dry out when exposed to sunlight or extreme heat. These factors can alter the stone's

Tyrone turquoise

color over time. Harder, gemstone-grade turquoise stones, which are rarer, are impervious to body oils and their color remains consistent over time.

Turquoise tends to form in arid, mountainous regions, such as those found in Persia, Central Asia, and the American Southwest. Deposits also occur in arid northern Africa, Australia, Siberia, and Europe.

In these regions, exposed rock surfaces are subjected to the erosive effects of periodic water runoff and rapid drying. Water flowing over exposed rock releases the chemical building blocks of turquoise, which are carried down in solution and ultimately accumulate and crystallize in fractures in the host rock. Over time, as the process of collecting and depositing these trace elements is repeated, the turquoise increases in density. The greater the stone's density, the deeper its color will tend to be.

Because of the wide variations possible in this mineral's density and its chemical makeup, turquoise can vary considerably in hue. Turquoise can range from a deep blue to a light green; sometimes blue and green are layered in the same stone.

The extent to which a particular stone is more or less blue or green depends upon the amount of copper content in its chemical chain. Generally speaking, stones with more copper content appear bluer, while those with less copper and more iron are greener. The specific mineralogical makeup of turquoise and perceived color also will vary according to the amount of pyrites, quartz, chert, and other minerals present in the matrix.

Turquoise veins in host rock

Deposits are most often located in igneous rocks, such as granite or trachyte, but veins of turquoise also have been found in metamorphic rocks, such as schist or gneiss; and some sedimentary rocks, such as shale, sandstone, and slate. The exact chemistry of a turquoise deposit can vary according to the deposition of other minerals in the host rock, such as quartz, iron pyrites, kaolin, manganite, and chalcedony. The presence of these other minerals also affects the stone's color and the character of its matrix.

Sleeping Beauty turquoise rough

Blue Gem turquoise veins in host rock

Most turquoise deposits lie no deeper than one hundred feet (thirty meters) below ground (although in some modern open pit copper mines such as the Lavender Pit in Bisbee, Arizona, turquoise deposits have been discovered as deep as two thousand feet). The earliest turquoise miners, who used stone mauls and did not have the technology to dig deep shafts, tended to concentrate on lower-quality, near-surface deposits. But the denser, and thus higher-grade, turquoise tends to form deeper underground in harder host rock, principally granite, and requires modern mining methods to extract.

Turquoise frequently occurs with other oxide copper minerals, such as chrysocolla, and sometimes near veins of silver or gold. Indeed, some of the largest turquoise veins are associated with huge open-pit copper mines such as those at Bisbee and Morenci, Arizona, and were rediscovered during the copper boom of the twentieth century.

Prospectors and geologists also know that turquoise deposits are found most often on the southern slopes of mountains. In winter, southern slopes receive more sunlight and snow tends to melt more rapidly there. Interestingly, the same runoff that forms turquoise also carries loose bits, called "float," into washes below. An alert rock hunter who finds some of this float might discover a rich turquoise deposit by following the runoff's path up the hillside to the source.

For modern-day miners, the urge to search for turquoise and the thrill of uncovering a new deposit of the blue and green colored rock within the crevices of a hillside remains as strong as ever. Unlike the earliest miners who labored with stone tools, miners today are equipped with steel shovels, jackhammers, backhoes, and bulldozers. The prospect of finding one more or better piece compels us to keep digging until it's too dark to see. Then, exhaustion competes with exhilaration, making it difficult to get a good night's sleep. Instead, we tend to toss and turn until first light, when we can grab our tools and start all over again, lest someone else discover the mother lode before we do.

Herculano Montoya at Tiffany Mine, Cerrillos, New Mexico ca. 1937

Joe Dan Lowry working at Enchantment Mine, Lincoln County, New Mexico ca. 1997

TURQUOISE AROUND THE WORLD

Throughout history, people of many cultures have prized turquoise's beautiful blues and greens for decoration and credited the gemstone with mystical and medicinal powers. For example, some in the Middle East believe a turquoise amulet can protect the wearer from the evil eye, accidents, venomous snakebites, scorpion stings, and disease. Other cultures believe the stone can help cure epilepsy, restore a person to sanity, and prevent blindness.

Persian turquoise

The ancient Egyptians may have been the first to mine turquoise. Jewelry encrusted with the stone has been found in five-thousand-year-old Egyptian tombs, and the oldest known turquoise mines were located in the Sinai Peninsula. One of these, at Serabit El-Khadem, may have been worked as early as 3500 B.C.

In the northern Neyshābūr region of Iran, turquoise is especially abundant and mines have been worked there since at least 2100 B.C. Indeed, statues of gods and goddesses inlaid with turquoise have been excavated from some of the most ancient archeological sites in Iran and neighboring Iraq. Persian turquoise is renowned and coveted for its clear, high-grade blue character. However, the Islamic Revolution in the early 1980s severely disrupted the production and distribution of Persian turquoise to Western markets.

Turquoise also has been mined in China for thousands of years, as evidenced by use of the gemstone in carvings dating from some of the earliest dynasties there. Since the 1980s, China has become the largest source, accounting for as much as half of today's worldwide turquoise trade.

Today, Chinese turquoise is more affordable than American turquoise because the supply is abundant, labor costs are lower, and there are fewer environmental restrictions governing mining in China. Colors vary greatly; the stones usually have a brown or black web matrix. Major deposits are found in the Hubei Province north of Xian.

Chinese turquoise

Some Chinese turquoise looks a lot like turquoise from "classic" American mines, and is often misrepresented as such. It is more common today to find Native American jewelry set with Chinese turquoise than with true Southwestern turquoise, so the buyer must beware. Given the law of supply and demand, and all other things being equal, a piece of Indian jewelry set with Chinese turquoise is worth a fraction of the value of an identical piece set with turquoise from one of the premiere Southwestern mines.

In the Western Hemisphere, significant deposits of turquoise have been found in Peru, Chile, and the Mexican states of Zacatecas and Sonora. Many of these sites were well known to the ancients and have been worked for a very long time. Most of the turquoise mined from these districts is soft and needs to be treated in order to be used in jewelry. The highest quality, gem-grade turquoise deposits in the Western Hemisphere occur in the arid American Southwest, particularly in the states of Nevada, Arizona, Colorado, and New Mexico.

TURQUOISE IN THE AMERICAN SOUTHWEST

Turquoise has been spiritually, decoratively, and economically significant to native peoples of what is now the American Southwest since at least A.D. 300, and perhaps earlier. Examples of worked turquoise dating from this Late Archaic period were found during initial archaeological excavations of Snaketown ruin, a major Hohokam site along the Gila River, south of Phoenix, Arizona, conducted in the 1930s by Emil Haury and Harold Gladwin. Subsequent excavations turned up numerous beads, pendants, mosaics, and ornamental overlays on bone dating to as late as A.D.1450.

In 1896, the Hyde Exploring Expedition conducted the first extensive, albeit highly controversial, archaeological excavations at Chaco Canyon in northwestern New Mexico. They found mosaic work, inlaid ritual objects, and tens of thousands of turquoise beads. During subsequent excavations, conducted between 1921 and 1927 by Neil M. Judd under the auspices of the National Geographic Society, more than 56,000 pieces were found in a single burial site at the Pueblo Bonito, the

Ancestral pueblo turquoise-inlaid jet frog (above) and turquoise beads (facing page) recovered from Pueblo Bonito in Chaco Canyon, New Mexico, by the Hyde Exploring Expedition, 1896.

largest of dozens of the magnificent, multistory "great houses" constructed by the ancestral people of Chaco. Another important collection of Chaco turquoise bead necklaces, uncovered at Shabik'eshchee, dates from A.D. 500.

In the 1990s, at Fajada Butte in Chaco, an archeological team supervised by Thomas Windes for the National Park Service found enormous quantities of raw, partly worked, and finished pieces of turquoise. The team concluded that a major workshop had operated there between approximately A.D. 950 and 1050, processing turquoise objects on a large scale, perhaps for trade.

The earliest examples of worked turquoise include nuggets and rough beads into which holes have been drilled to create simple necklaces and earrings. Around A.D.1300, the Hohokam people of what is now southern Arizona began to create more refined mosaic jewelry and ceremonial objects by gluing chips of turquoise to wood, bone, and shell bases.

These techniques were subsequently adopted by the Hopi, Zuni, and other Pueblo peoples

Ancestral pueblo turquoise mosaic cylinder (facing page) and necklace (top) found at Pueblo Bonito in Chaco Canyon, New Mexico. Prehistoric Hohokam turquoise and hematite mosaic earrings (above) excavated from Snaketown, Arizona.

of what is now northern Arizona and New Mexico. Archaeologist Frederick Hodge found examples dating from the late sixteenth or early seventeenth centuries near Zuni Pueblo between 1917 and 1920. Among the objects he uncovered were combs and pieces of mosaic jewelry made from wood and seashells to which bits of turquoise had been glued with pinyon pine pitch. Today, artisans of Zuni and Santo Domingo pueblos use similar techniques and materials to create their artwork

THE PREHISTORIC TURQUOISE TRADE

During this prehistoric period, turquoise mined in the American Southwest was exchanged with peoples residing as far east as the Mississippi River, and trade also extended west and south to the Pacific Coast and Gulf of California. Some of the earliest jewelry found at archaeological sites on the Colorado plateau combined blue or green turquoise with seashell, most notably the red *Spondylus,* or spiny oyster, which is found off the coast of California.

Prehistoric Sinagua turquoise-inlaid shell pendant found at Montezuma Castle, Arizona.

Based on the large quantities of turquoise artifacts uncovered at several major archeological sites in Mexico, Guatemala, and Honduras, it appears the Mayan and Aztec cultures were as fond of *chalchihuitl* as the Pueblo cultures of the American Southwest. And, like the nomadic Apaches, the Aztecs must have believed in turquoise's protective powers, because they studded their shields and ceremonial masks with it.

Although the Mexican districts of La Barranca and Santa Rosa have significant turquoise deposits, they are not believed to be the sole sources of turquoise found in excavated sites in Central America. The indigenous peoples of Mexico had plenty of parrot and macaw feathers, copper bells, seashells, and other exotic trade items they could exchange for the turquoise they craved. In fact, such trade items have been found in many ancient settlements throughout the American Southwest, most notably in Chaco Canyon and Pecos Pueblo in New Mexico.

Quantities of turquoise objects found in ancient burial sites throughout the American Southwest confirm that the stone had spiritual significance for ancestral Pueblo people, and turquoise is important to their descendants as well. The Zuni and peoples of the Rio Grande pueblos associate blue turquoise with Father Sky and green turquoise with Mother Earth. Early Zuni fetishes were made of turquoise, or at least had turquoise eyes, mouths, or attachments to enhance their power. Zuni and Hopi katsina dancers wear turquoise necklaces, and powdered turquoise is a common offering to accompany a prayer.

Ancestral pueblo medicine bag

COPR. FRED HARVEY

H-1951 AN OLD NAVAJO INDIAN MEDICINE MAN, NEW MEXICO

Other native peoples of the American Southwest, including the Navajo, Apaches and Pima, believe turquoise is imbued with special powers. The Navajos believe turquoise jewelry will bring good fortune to the wearer and curry favor with the Ye'iis, beings who mediate between mortals and the spirit world. Apache hunters and warriors once attached bits of turquoise to their bows to make arrows fly straight and true, and wore turquoise as protection against enemies. The Pima carried turquoise to ward off illness.

PREHISTORIC MINING
Archaeologists have identified more than two hundred prehistoric turquoise-mining sites. One of the best known is on Mount Chalchihuitl in New Mexico's Cerrillos district. It was worked by the people of San Marcos Pueblo, whose descendants now occupy Santo Domingo, from approximately A.D. 1300 until the arrival of the Spanish in the 1500s. Unlike most Southwestern mines of the period, this was an underground mine with tunnels connecting shafts as deep as two hundred feet. Notched ladder logs were found at the site, along with stone mauls and broken pieces of pottery.

SPANISH CONTACT
After their conquest of the Aztecs in Mexico in the early 1500s, Spanish explorers led by Francisco Vásquez de Coronado arrived in the American Southwest in 1540, lured by reports of abundant mineral wealth, especially gold. Finding none, the Spanish had little immediate incentive to establish a permanent presence there. Not until 1598 did the first Spanish missionaries and colonists arrive to settle.

In due course, the Spanish seized the Pueblo turquoise mines in the Cerrillos Hills and forced the people of San Marcos Pueblo to work them. History suggests that this practice, coupled with tragic cave-ins, helped fuel the Pueblo Revolt of 1680, during which the Spanish missionaries and colonists were forced to flee south to what is now El Paso, Texas.

In 1692, the Spanish returned to reassert their control of New Mexico, and by the late 1700s their influence had spread as far west as southern Nevada. Welcome or not, the Spanish nevertheless brought with them horses, cattle, sheep, and farming methods that would profoundly transform life for the native peoples of the American Southwest. The Spanish also introduced metal mining and smithing tools, and other iron, silver, tin, and copper objects and materials that the native population, Navajos in particular, could rework for their own purposes.

Navajo Silver and Tyrone turquoise Spanish-style spur pendants

Herculano Montoya at Tiffany Mine, Cerrillos, New Mexico ca. 1937

THE AMERICAN ERA

Mexico gained its independence from Spain in 1821, which brought the territory from modern Texas to California under Mexican control. In 1847, the United States declared war on Mexico and took possession of the northern half of Mexico's territory in North America. In 1849, gold was discovered in California, and the rush was on. By the 1870s, mining towns had sprung up not just in California but throughout the intermountain American West. Miners found large deposits of copper, lead, silver, gold, and turquoise, which frequently appeared in the same ore bodies.

I-56   Navajo Girl Proud of Her Jewelry

Some miners looked exclusively for turquoise. Dedicated turquoise mining operations tended to be small-scale. Prospectors worked with minimal equipment, strong backs, and passionate ambitions. In this period, miners used explosives in addition to hand tools to crack open rocks.

Coincident with the boom in turquoise mining, artisans in Zuni, Rio Grande pueblos, and Navajo country learned metalsmithing. A Zuni craftsman named Kineshde is believed to have been the first to add turquoise to the metal objects he made, thus creating a new art form. The arrival of the transcontinental Atchison, Topeka, and Santa Fe Railway in northern New Mexico and Arizona in the early 1880s helped spark interest in authentic, handcrafted silver and turquoise Indian jewelry. Settlers and tourists from the East, and California, were captivated by this uniquely American art form, and this trade provided impoverished native peoples of the American Southwest with much-needed income.

As artisans refined their skills and consumer interest in Native American jewelry grew, so too did the demand for artists, silver, and turquoise. Popular books such as Joseph Pogue's classic *The Turquois*,

Jeweler Zuni Dick, ca. 1935

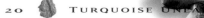

In Zuni, ca. 1950, youth learned jewelry-making skills and helped revive the Indian jewelry trade.

first published in 1915, helped create international interest in, and demand for, quality turquoise Indian jewelry.

After World War II, the population in the American Southwest exploded, and so too did tourism to the region, thanks largely to a booming automobile culture and a strong U.S. economy. Interest in and demand for turquoise, and turquoise Indian jewelry in particular, expanded exponentially. The federal government even established programs to teach the jewelry making trades to budding Native American artisans. J.C. "Zack" and Donald Zachary were recruited in the 1950s to establish one such school on the Cañoncito (now Tò Hajilee) Navajo Reservation.

Underscoring the importance of turquoise to the economic and spiritual well-being of native peoples in the American Southwest, both New Mexico and Arizona recognize it as the state gem, and Nevada has designated it as the semiprecious state gem.

It is much more expensive to mine turquoise today than in the heyday of the twentieth century. Labor and machinery costs are higher, government worker safety laws are more restrictive, and environmental regulations require miners to reclaim and restore their land once mining operations have ceased. But the growing market for Southwestern turquoise is reviving interest in old deposits and intensifying the search for new ones. Some of the classic Southwestern mines are still active and others are being reopened. A few claims that once produced lovely turquoise have been leased or sold to gold and copper mining companies and are not accessible to turquoise miners.

Blue Gem nugget and bead necklace

WORKING WITH TURQUOISE

The earliest native peoples shaped the turquoise they quarried into rough beads or into simple shapes that could be affixed to shell, bone, or wood. More recently the stone has been magnificently matched with all sorts of metals, especially silver. How does one take a rough rock that has just a hint of pretty color and is sold by the pound and turn it into a polished gem that is colorfully complex and sold by the carat?

CUTTING AND POLISHING
Finishing turquoise requires the skill of cutters (lapidaries), who turn chunks of turquoise ore into polished stones in a series of steps.

Vein formations typically range from the width of a cornflake to a quarter-inch thick. Turquoise may also emerge from a mine as a nugget, as small as a fingernail or as big as an egg. Some nuggets have weighed as much as twenty-five pounds. To be workable, nuggets must be sliced into smaller pieces in a process called slabbing.

Almost all turquoise is cut as a doublet, or a layered stone, in which thin pieces are sandwiched with quick-drying epoxy and filler. The resulting doublets are more substantial and thus easier to cut and set. The final shape of a particular piece of turquoise is largely determined from the shape of its slab or doublet. Sometimes the process of cutting soft turquoise leaves pits, which may be filled with materials such as epoxy to create a smoother surface.

Natural turquoise doublets set on dopsticks
ready to be worked by a lapidary

Weighing raw turquoise at the Zuni Craftsman Co-op

Sanding and polishing turquoise

Next, the lapidary decides whether to preserve the stone's irregular shape or cut it to fit an oval or marquis setting. The latter require use of templates, with the excess turquoise being trimmed away. The resulting blank still may look rough, with notched edges that are removed during the grinding process later.

The blank is next attached with hot wax or wood glue to a six-inch wooden dowel, or "dop," in a step called dopping. This makes the blank easier to handle for shaping and polishing.

Grinding and sanding steps follow. Both processes happen on wheels fitted with progressively finer abrasive surfaces, ranging from 100 grit carborundum to very fine sandpaper. During grinding and sanding, the lapidary continually moistens the turquoise with water because stones may fragment if they become too hot or dry. After grinding the stone into its finished shape, the lapidary uses increasingly fine sandpaper to smooth the stone.

Once the stone has been ground and sanded to the lapidary's satisfaction, it is ready to be polished with a damp piece of leather or felt, water, and usually a tin-oxide cream. At this stage, a gem-grade stone will take on a high-gloss finish. A lesser-grade natural stone will exhibit a dull luster rather than a high shine. Once polished, the stone is removed from its dop and is ready to be set.

Grinding turquoise to template

SETTING THE STONE

Artisans tend to choose a piece of turquoise first and then create a setting to suit it. Most turquoise featured in this way is set within a bezel, which is a metal band shaped to fit the outline of the stone exactly. The bezel is soldered to a base of flat silver that also has been cut to fit the stone's shape. The bezel and base create a cuplike container that will hold the stone snugly.

Turquoise is often mounted with a backing or some other form of padding to give the stone greater height in its setting. The bezel is pressed smoothly and firmly against the turquoise with a simple tool to anchor it in place. Stones mounted in this manner may have a somewhat domed (cabochon) surface.

Silver and Lander Blue turquoise earrings

Most Navajo turquoise jewelry employs the bezel technique. Heavy silver pieces with large stones, the concha belt, the "squash blossom" necklace, the use of silver beads, and the bola necktie are all typical of classic Navajo design.

Artists from Zuni pueblo are masters of the inlay technique in jewelry design, in which turquoise and other materials (such as coral, jet, and mother-of-pearl) are set in epoxy on a flat silver base with surrounding bezel to create a pictorial or abstract mosaic design. Zuni jewelers also are celebrated for their petit point and needle point work.

In a variation called channel inlay, thin strips of silver are soldered perpendicular to a larger silver base. Pieces of turquoise are then carefully cut to fit tightly in the channels between the silver strips. The silver is then ground level with the turquoise to give the effect of a bezel. Alternatively, stones may be mounted with glue. However, this is an inferior method because glue has a tendency to deteriorate over time and stones may eventually fall out of their settings.

Zuni turquoise channel inlay technique

Zuni jeweler Della Casi, ca. 1935

Hopi jewelry makers are renowned for creating silver overlay pieces, in which stencil-cut sheets of silver are affixed to silver bases to create a shadowbox effect. Turquoise, coral, and other stones can be mounted in the open spaces of the upper layer's design.

Santo Domingo jewelers prefer to emulate the ancient methods of setting turquoise, before silver came into use. They are renowned for stringing necklaces with rough nuggets and heishi beads.

The latter are created by segmenting a thin, flat square of turquoise into a grid and drilling a hole in the center of each section. Each square is then rounded into a cylindrically-shaped bead. Santo Domingo artisans also glue shell-and-turquoise mosaics on wood, just as their ancestors did.

Zuni silver, turquoise, and shell pendant

*A*tsidi Sani ("Old Smith"), a Navajo man who learned metalsmithing ca. 1870 from a Mexican ironsmith called Nakai Tsos, may have been the first Native American to practice the craft. He passed his skills on to his sons, who in turn taught others. Early Navajo metalsmiths used discarded metal objects, including silver U.S. dollars and Mexican pesos, to create objects such as horse bridle headstalls, hairpins, and moccasin buttons.

By 1872, metalsmithing found its way to Zuni, and artisans there may have been the first in the Southwest to combine silver with turquoise. Today, almost every Native American community in the Southwest has its distinctive, recognizable style of jewelry.

Navajo silver and turquoise concha

Rolled turquoise beads

BUYING TURQUOISE

Mineralogists, geologists, miners, and other experts in the turquoise industry continue to develop and refine a qualitative system for rating turquoise. The primary variables they consider are density (hardness), depth of color, and the stone's matrix. Informed consumers should also consider the relative rarity of a particular piece of turquoise in relation to all other qualitative factors that determine a stone's value.

Today, many collectors are very interested to know exactly where a particular piece of turquoise was mined in order to better appreciate its value. But others are more interested in finding that special piece with a certain shape, color, and matrix that "speaks" to them. Other collectors concentrate on buying wonderful examples of jewelry: A magnificent setting can add value to a stone by showing it off to best advantage.

To those of us in the trade, the most valuable turquoise is exceptionally dense and has deep colors, a complex matrix, and a pedigree from "classic" mines in the American Southwest—such as Lone Mountain, Number 8, Lander Blue, and Bisbee—where production has ceased.

But for you, the consumer, the choice is really a matter of personal taste: Ultimately, the "best" turquoise is that which most appeals to you. And the better informed you are about the variety of options available, the more satisfied you are likely to be with your purchase decision.

Navajo silver belt buckle set with Turquoise Mountain turquoise

DENSITY
Density is the most important factor to consider because it largely determines the stone's color, depth, and brilliance as well as its ability to be worked. About fifteen percent of all turquoise is hard enough to be considered gem grade. The finest, densest grades of turquoise—also among the rarest—have deep, brilliant shades of blues and greens that can be as breathtaking as a clear spring sky or as lush as a mountain meadow. Lower-grade turquoise, which is more common, is less dense, less colorful, and less durable. But every grade and shade of turquoise has its own special character, and many people actually favor the rugged, "ancient" appearance of lower-grade stones.

The lowest grade turquoise is soft enough to write with on a chalkboard. It can only be used commercially when treated with waxes and oils or stabilized with plastic. Similarly, turquoise chips that are too small to be worked can be reconstituted and shaped into a hardened block. It is even possible to replicate spider web matrix patterns in both stabilized and reconstituted turquoise. Most turquoise marketed today has been treated.

Zuni inlay bracelet with stabilized turquoise

COLOR AND CLARITY
Many in the industry claim that certain colors of turquoise are "better" than others. Perhaps the most common misconception is that blue turquoise is more valuable than green. A blue stone with a spiderweb matrix is worth more than a green stone, but a green stone from the Blue Gem mine is worth more than a high grade blue Sleeping Beauty stone. Mine and matrix matter more than color. The law of supply and demand determines comparative market value.

Middle Eastern, European, and Asian collectors favor turquoise with exceptional clarity, i.e. stones that are uniformly colored and without impurities. Stones of this type are commonly described as "robin's egg." To achieve the prized unblemished look, the host rock may be sawed to eliminate any trace of matrix from the finished stone, or the stone may be shaped in a way that hides its impurities. Iran has historically been a good source for robin's egg turquoise, although mines there have produced beautiful matrix turquoise as well.

Persian "robin's egg" turquoise

MATRIX

While some may regard intrusions from the host rock and the presence of other minerals in turquoise as impurities, others see this matrix as the very thing that gives each stone its unique character and signature. Depending on the composition of the host rock, a matrix may be golden, brown, black, white, or even sienna. What may appear to be gold in the matrix is usually iron or copper pyrites (fool's gold).

Some matrices are more desirable to collectors than others. One person might perceive the matrix of a particular stone to be ugly, while another will find the same stone exotic and beautiful. In terms of grading, a stone in which the matrix pattern is evenly distributed is more valuable than a one with an uneven, "blotchy" matrix. Of the various types of matrices, "spider web" is the rarest and most sought-after. This matrix, also referred to as "eggshell," is made up of a web-like network of thin lines. Mines that are particularly noted for producing fine spider web turquoise are Number 8, Lone Mountain, and Lander Blue.

Number 8, renowned for fine "spider web" matrix

RARITY

A mine that produces a limited amount of ore can command a higher price for its turquoise. The Lander Blue Mine produced no more than one hundred eight pounds of extremely high-grade turquoise with a fine matrix, and today Lander Blue commands the highest prices per carat weight.

Lander Blue, the most valuable per carat weight

There are exceptions. One turquoise deposit, Weird Clear, produced only two full buckets. As rare as it is, Weird Clear is soft and pale and has little value.

Natural turquoise is rarer than treated turquoise and is priced accordingly. Other qualities, such as the history or size of a particular piece, can make a stone rare in the eyes of certain collectors. A medium-quality stone from a closed mine with a particularly colorful history may command a higher price than an equally good stone from an active mine without such an interesting (or advertised) past. Knowledgeable buyers will gladly pay a premium for turquoise with a provenance. Similarly, an unusually large turquoise nugget is likely to attract the attention of collectors, even if the turquoise itself is only of medium grade.

The complex character of natural turquoise is revealed in this example from the Stormy Mountain Mine.

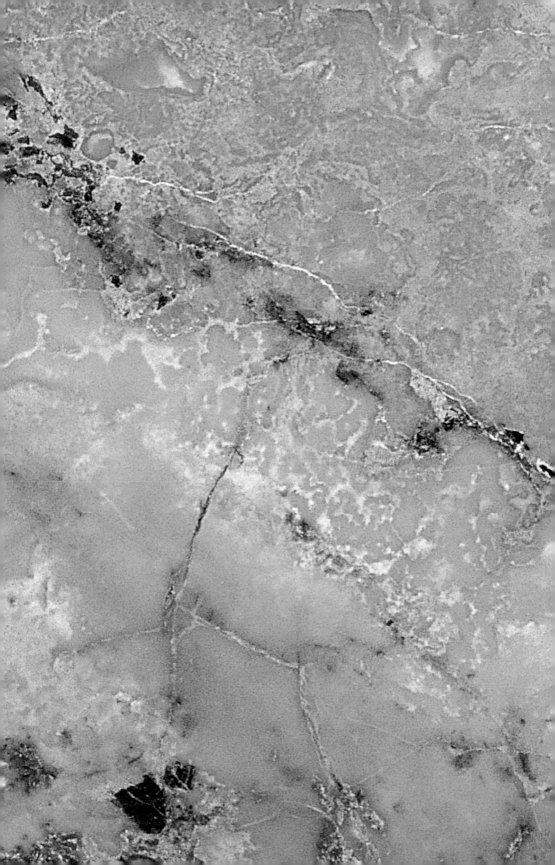

TREATED TURQUOISE
Natural, gemstone-grade turquoise, which has enough density, size, and color to be cut, polished, and set in jewelry, represents only about 15 percent of all turquoise available on the market. The far larger percentage of turquoise is lower grade and must be treated in some way to make it commercially usable. Turquoise is considered "treated," rather than natural, if it has been:

Dyed, in which blue, green, or yellow pigment is added to deepen a stone's color.

Reconstituted, in which chips or fragments are pulverized, and the resulting powder is mixed with epoxy to form hard cakes or blocks that can be cut into "stones."

Stabilized, in which low-grade or chalk turquoise is combined with a colorless acrylic or another plastic bonding agent under pressure or in a vacuum to harden the material and darken the color.

Enhanced, in which the structure of a low- or medium-grade stone is improved through a patented process.

Oiled or waxed, in which the stone is soaked or "cooked" to deepen its color.

Dealers should also inform the buyer if a stone's matrix has been dyed, if pits have been filled and smoothed, if it is doublet cut, or if it has been sawed with an oil-based compound, which could alter the color of the turquoise. Treating low-grade turquoise may make it more attractive and salable, but it is not worth as much as a natural, unadulterated gemstone and should be priced accordingly.

chalk

stabilized

natural low grade

natural low grade

stabilized

chalk

waxed

stabilized

reconstituted

IMITATION TURQUOISE
In some cases, material represented and sold as turquoise is actually colored plastic. Real minerals, such as howlite and quartzite, are sometimes dyed to imitate natural turquoise and can be hard to detect as fake.

Other stones simply look a lot like the real thing. Several of these so-called "turquoise family" minerals have similar chemical formulas, form in rocks in a similar way, and have a similar crystalline structure. Because turquoise is more marketable, these stones are sometimes sold as turquoise, which is a pity because they are very attractive in their own right:

Chalcosiderite (kalkohSIDerite) is a whitish mineral also known by the common name New Lander.

Chrysocolla (kriSOHkola) is a hard, green-blue mineral, the colors of which often vary widely in the same specimen

Faustite (FAWStite), is an apple-green-colored mineral which forms alongside turquoise in the Carico Lake area of Nevada and other locations.

Variscite (VEHrihsite), ranges from light to dark green with nice webbing.

Malachite (MALuhkite) *and Azurite* (ASyurite) are copper ores. Like turquoise, these are also cut and polished for jewelry, and their blue and green colors and the areas where they are found are almost the same as for turquoise.

GET IT IN WRITING
How can you protect yourself from misrepresentations? The best way is to obtain proper written documentation of your purchase. Turquoise dealers are required by law to accurately and truthfully represent the stones they sell, and they must fully disclose the condition of each stone. Federal Trade Commission guidelines strongly suggest that buyers obtain a receipt that includes all the vital information about the value of their purchase, including verbal representations. For example, if the seller tells you that the turquoise jewelry you're buying is sterling silver and natural turquoise, and was handmade by a Native American artisan, you should ask that this information be spelled out on your receipt. A reputable dealer will not hesitate to give you a detailed written confirmation.

Santo Domingo necklaces with stabilized turquoise

Dendrite turquoise

Dendrite turquoise is exceedingly rare.
The fern-like pattern in the matrix
is produced by the crystallization of
a foreign mineral, usually an oxide of
manganese, at the time the turquoise
itself is being formed.

Fossil turquoise

Turquoise fossils occur when turquoise
minerals migrate to and replace the
original calcium-rich skeletal material
of primordial, long-buried plants or animals.

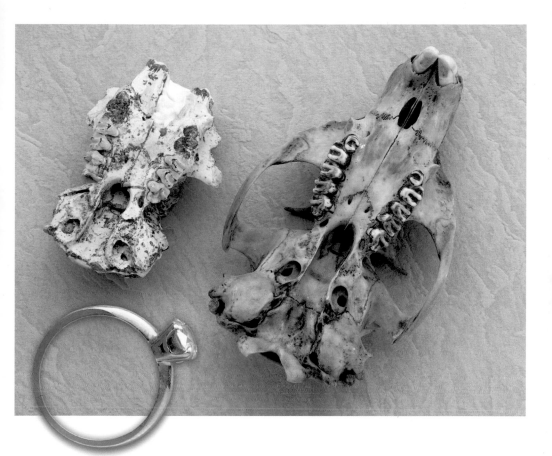

Fossil turquoise

Tiny turquoise teeth adorn the fossilized upper jaw (left) of an ancient yellow-bellied marmot (*Marmora flaviventris*). This chunky rodent once lived in caves in the Potosi Mountains of Nevada, southwest of Las Vegas. Thousands of years spent soaking in ground water rich in copper transformed the enamel of the marmot's teeth into pure turquoise and the soft inner dentine into a different mineral called calcite. Other traces of copper can be seen in the pale bluish-white color of the skull, which also turned to calcite. A modern marmot skull (right) from the Sierra Nevada shows what parts of the fossilized skull are missing. Near the marmot jaw, fossil hunters also discovered the turquoise jaw of a prehistoric ringtail cat and some ancient turquoise camel teeth.

Classic Southwestern Turquoise Mines

While turquoise deposits are found all over the world, fewer than three dozen sites, all located in the American Southwest, are widely recognized in the turquoise trade as "classic mines." Stones unearthed from each of these named deposits have a well-documented pedigree and can be easily identified by their characteristic colors and matrix.

Although the quality of turquoise from these sites can be exceptional, the output from some is relatively small and the supply of stones from others is dwindling. To determine the true worth of a turquoise stone, therefore, one must consider its rarity as well as its unique color, matrix, and origin. The rarest turquoise tends to command the highest prices.

For example, the Sleeping Beauty mine in Arizona and the Carico Lake mine in Nevada provide the turquoise jewelry industry—individual artists as well as large-scale manufacturers—with a steady supply of stones that are consistent in color and price. The Number 8 Mine in Nevada, on the other hand, has not been mined since 1961, and thus the availability of stones from this site is very limited. Because of its rarity, a medium-grade Number 8

< **Bisbee** Bisbee turquoise is a significant by-product of the huge Lavender Pit copper mine, which is now closed. Bisbee turquoise is famous for its deep blue color and its smoky black matrix, which has been described as "smoky Bisbee" and as "lavender." (Navajo squash blossom necklace and bracelet) *Cochise County, Arizona*

stone is worth considerably more than a high-grade piece of comparable weight from either Sleeping Beauty or Carico Lake.

Today's turquoise claims are identified by name, although certain names have changed over time. Sixty years ago, the Tyrone mine in New Mexico and the Fox mine in Nevada were known as the Azure and Cortez mines, respectively. At that time, J.W. Edgar and C.G. Wallace were busy mining and marketing turquoise to supply to the developing turquoise Indian jewelry industry.

Since the 1960s, mine owners such as Dowell Ward and Eddy Mauzy have continued these traditions of salesmanship and product promotion. They knew intuitively that amusing or historic anecdotes, an established history, quality stones, and a certain available supply could propel a mine to the forefront of the turquoise industry.

Miners and legendary turquoise entrepreneurs like J. W. Edgar, J.C. Zachary, Jr., Dowell Ward, and Eddy Mauzy were never short of stories and opinions about turquoise; they were naturally passionate about the subject—you could say they lived this passion. But despite the many colorful yarns they all spun about turquoise and turquoise mining, they could not have imagined how significant the American turquoise industry would become by the end of the twentieth century, nor could they have imagined that one day the whole world would be caught up in turquoise's romantic and ever-expanding web.

> **Lander Blue**   Rita J. Hapgood, a blackjack dealer at the Nevada Club at Battle Mountain, discovered this turquoise deposit in 1973 while picnicking at Indian Creek. Drawn to a bird's nest, she also noticed some unusual black rocks studded with blue dots that were like none she had ever seen before. She collected some of these nuggets in a coffee can and later claimed the site as the Mary Louise Lode Mining Claim. Later that year, she sold her claim to Marvin Syme and Henry Dorian, who formed the Lander Blue Turquoise Corporation. With an old tractor and a compressor contributed by Bob Johnson, the partners worked the claim for a year until the deposit of extraordinary turquoise ran out.

Lander Blue was a "hat mine," so called because you could cover it with a hat. Today, this rarest of all Southwestern turquoise "classics" is also of the highest grade and thus, pound for pound, the most valuable turquoise in the world. (Navajo petit point squash blossom nedcklace and earring set, rings, and bracelet)
Lander County, Nevada

∧ **Morenci** This turquoise is highly sought after for its blue colors and iron pyrite, or "fool's gold," matrix. The name derives from the large open-pit Morenci copper mine. A great deal of turquoise from Morenci has been of the "lunch box" variety, spirited out of the pit in lunch boxes by sharp-eyed heavy-equipment operators and miners. (Navajo bracelets; Zuni belt buckle) *Greenlee County, Arizona*

< **Lone Mountain** This mine once produced a great variety of turquoise, including some of the finest examples of spider web turquoise as well as clear, deep-blue stones. Among all "classic" Southwestern turquoise, only Lander Blue is more valuable. The Lone Mountain mine consists of a series of haphazard tunnels dug by miners chasing veins of "blue gold." As the veins played out, the mine became less cost effective and increasingly dangerous to operate. (Navajo bone knife handle and bola tie) *Esmeralda County, Nevada*

∧ **Sleeping Beauty**   A heavy producer of copper ore, the Sleeping Beauty mine also produces remarkably uniform blue turquoise that is easily matched or cut into sets and used in many styles of Indian jewelry, including Zuni needlepoint and inlay pieces. Sleeping Beauty's matrix is generally white and dyed black using shoe polish. Sleeping Beauty turquoise is relatively abundant and thus more affordable, making this "classic" one of the few actively exported to markets in Asia, Europe, and the Middle East. (Zuni inlay bola tie and earrings) *Gila County, Arizona*

> **Number 8**   This large district, encompassing ten 20-acre claims, was very active from the 1930s through the early 1950s, when production peaked. Lee Hand, the Edgar family, and Dowell Ward were involved in developing it. Number 8 is famous for its black, golden, red, and brown spider-web varieties, which are defining characteristics of the "classic" turquoise. Some enormous nodules were unearthed from this area, including one that weighed 150 pounds. (Navajo concha belt, bracelet, and pendant; Santo Domingo nugget necklace) *Eureka County, Nevada*

∧ **Fox** Fox is one of Nevada's most productive mines. Dowell Ward purchased the old Cortez claims in the 1940s and developed them using the names Fox, White Horse, Green Tree, and Smith to differentiate among the colors of turquoise produced in the area, and to create a larger perceived share of the turquoise market. Collectively, the area produces a huge quantity of good-quality green or blue-green stone with a distinctive matrix. (Navajo necklace, rings, and bracelet) *Lander County, Nevada*

> **Blue Gem** This mine, which is no longer active, produced almost every shade of green and blue turquoise imaginable. Blue Gem was located about six miles south of Battle Mountain, within a large copper-mining operation. Of the several Nevada mines that are named Blue Gem, this is the largest and most famous. (Santo Domingo nugget and bead necklaces; Navajo bracelets) *Lander County, Nevada*

< **Kingman** Copper mining in the Mineral Park Mining District around Kingman has produced a large supply of turquoise through the years. The matrix of most Kingman turquoise is naturally white but is usually dyed to black with shoe polish. (Zuni nugget and shell bead necklace) *Mohave County, Arizona*

∧ **Cripple Creek** Miners looking for gold in the Cripple Creek area also found turquoise deposits. There are two separate mines that are currently active in the area. Although they have been operated by different families, both mines market their turquoise under the Cripple Creek name and supply a variety of colors and matrices primarily to the Indian jewelry industry. (Zuni fetishes) *Teller County, Colorado*

∧ **King's Manassa** This site, originally mined by Ancestral Pueblo peoples, was rediscovered in 1890 by gold prospector I.P. King, and his descendents still work the claim. King's Manassa turquoise is best known for its brilliant greens and golden matrices, but blue and blue-green turquoise was found amid these deposits as well. (Navajo belt buckle, ring, and bracelets) *Conejos County, Colorado*

J. W. Edgar made a living doing a lot of things, from breaking horses to selling automobiles, but he loved turquoise prospecting most of all. He was living in Colorado in the late 1920s when his brother wrote from Tonopah, Nevada, to say he'd seen "turquoise all over the ground" there. J.W. promptly packed his pickup truck and headed west.

One of the men J.W. met when he arrived in Nevada was August "Gus" Stenich, an elderly Austrian immigrant who owned a gold mine with significant turquoise deposits, as well as a turquoise mine that became known as Carico Lake. Over the years, Gus had lost many pounds of turquoise to scavengers and cheats, so he had a reputation as a suspicious and ornery character. But Gus trusted the younger J.W. like he was his own son, and the two became close friends.

Gus was a loner who preferred to work his claims by himself. Even so, J.W. worried about his friend spending so much time "out there" alone and made a point to check up on Gus from time to time. One day J.W. arrived at his friend's tent camp to find his worst fears realized. Gus had died, but not before making out his will on a wrinkled paper bread wrapper, which J.W. found clutched in the old man's hand. His last thoughts had been of his one true friend, and he had left all that he owned to the one man in the world he trusted: J.W. Edgar.

> ## Carico Lake
Carico Lake is a relatively large, active mining district encompassing several claims that produce a variety of graded blue and green turquoise. Turquoise from the Carico Lake district has been marketed under several other names, including Aurora and Stone Cabin. Mines in this district also produce faustite, an apple-green mineral similar to turquoise, but incorporating zinc rather than copper. Faustite was identified as a separate mineral in 1953. (Navajo bola tie; Zuni inlay earrings) *Lander County, Nevada*

NOTICE OF LOCATION

Notice is hereby given that the undersigned hereby locate___ and claim___ the following described piece of mineral bearing ground as a __Turquoise__ claim.

From this discovery monument __750__ feet in a __Northerly__ direction and __750__ feet in a __Southerly__ direction, and three hundred feet on each side of the middle of the vein.

__Situated about 5 miles__
__Westerly from Carico Lake__
_____ and _____

The general course of the vein or ledge is __North__
_____ and __Southerly__ and the size of the claim is __1500__ feet long
__600__ feet wide. This claim shall be known as
the __Aurora No 1__
__Bullion__ situated in
__Lander__ Mining District
ed this __14__ day of __July__ County, Nevada 19__41__

__August Stenech__

LOCATOR

∧ **Enchantment**   In 1958, a gold prospector "rediscovered" a turquoise deposit near Ruidoso in Lincoln County, New Mexico, first identified on an 1895 map as "old Indian diggings." His find remained a well-kept secret until 1997, when he visited the Turquoise Museum. When he asked why the museum did not display any turquoise from Lincoln County, he was told that there were no known deposits there. He returned a week later with samples. The Lowry family subsequently acquired the claim, and today the Lost Mine of Enchantment produces medium-grade, yet authentically "New Mexican," turquoise to the Indian jewelry trade. (Santo Domingo necklace) *Lincoln County, New Mexico*

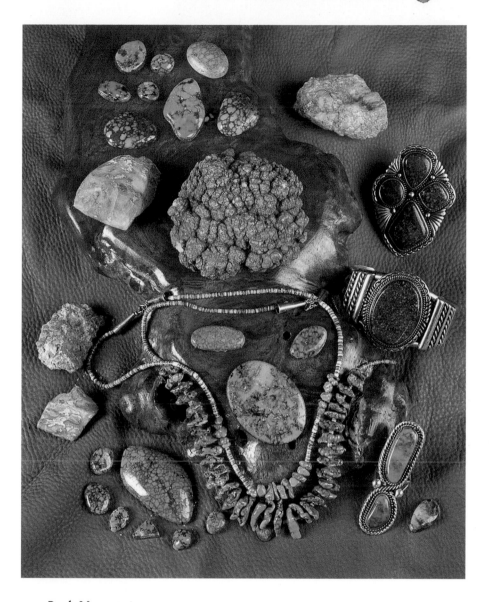

∧ **Red Mountain** Over the years this mine has produced a large quantity of graded turquoise, but the best Red Mountain turquoise rivals some of the higher quality material produced by the best mines in the Southwest. Red Mountain is a good source for intricate, spiderweb-matrix stones, many of which are used in the finest gold and silver Indian jewelry. The mine is also a popular source for small, high-grade nuggets that can be drilled, polished, and strung to make wonderful necklaces. (Santo Domingo nugget and heishi bead necklaces; Navajo ring, bracelet, pendant) *Lander County, Nevada*

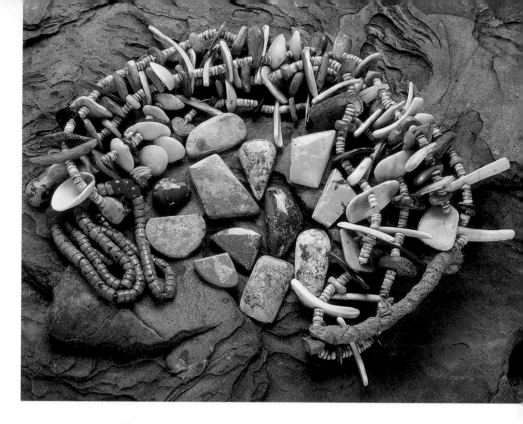

∧ Cerrillos

Located between Santa Fe and Albuquerque, New Mexico, Cerrillos is one of the most famous prehistoric mining districts in the American Southwest. Pueblo peoples mined the area extensively between A.D. 1300 and 1600. Of the more than two hundred dig sites located there, the largest and most famous are the Blue Bell, Castilian, and Tiffany mines. Large-scale commercial mining activity in the Cerrillos area wound down in the 1950s, but occasionally rock hounds and small mining claimholders still find small quantities of the relatively low-grade turquoise there. (Santo Domingo necklace) *Santa Fe County, New Mexico*

< Tyrone

Miner John Coleman is credited with rediscovering these ancient workings while on a hunting trip in the 1880s. The name "Tyrone" refers not to a specific turquoise but rather to the group of claims around Silver City and the Tyrone copper mine. The most famous of these was the Azure mine, which yielded the most valuable, bright blue turquoise ever found in New Mexico. The Elizabeth Pocket, discovered in the Azure mine in 1893, was the richest single vein of turquoise ever, measuring one hundred feet long, forty feet wide, and forty-five feet high. These mines offered some of New Mexico's finest turquoise, resembling both Persian and Bisbee turquoise in color and matrix. The host rocks lent pretty golden and brown webbing to the stones. Turquoise from the Cameo deposit was pure blue. (Navajo bola tie) *Grant County, New Mexico*

∧ **Pilot Mountain** This active mine currently produces a large
amount of graded turquoise with a variety of colors ranging
from blue to green with dark brown, black, or reddish matrices.
Deposits here consist primarily of thin seams with some nugget
formations. (Navajo bracelets) *Esmeralda County, Nevada*

> **Turquoise Mountain** Located in the Mineral Park Mining District,
Turquoise Mountain offers distinctive stones with unique blue and green
colors. Although Turquoise Mountain is located near the Kingman
deposits, it is considered a classic mine in its own right because
its turquoise is so different in appearance. Product from Turquoise
Mountain has also been sold as Old Man Turquoise. (Navajo
concha belt, ring, and belt buckle) *Mohave County, Arizona*

∧ Stormy Mountain

This mine, along with the Blue Diamond mine, is distinctive for producing hard, dark blue turquoise that includes a blotchy, black chert matrix that resembles storm clouds, hence the name Stormy Mountain. The mine is not presently active. (Navajo jewelry box) *Elko county, Nevada*

< Royston

Royston, originally known as the Royal Blue mine, produced turquoise that had a mixture of blues and greens in the same formation. There are several deposits in the Royston area that could still be profitably mined. (Navajo necklace and bracelets) *Nye County, Nevada*

> Indian Mountain

The best known of the contemporary mines originally discovered by a Native American. The lode was discovered in 1970 by a Shoshone sheepherder who stumbled upon a vein of turquoise on a hillside while tending his sheep. Eddy Mauzy and his family subsequently mined and marketed turquoise from this site to top Southwest Indian artisans, and jewelry featuring turquoise from Indian Mountain was first featured prominently in *Arizona Highways* magazine in the late 1970s. (Yaqui necklace; Hopi ring) *Lander County, Nevada*

MUSEUMS AND COLLECTIONS

Arizona State Museum Located on the campus of the University of Arizona in Tucson, this is the oldest and largest anthropology museum in the Southwest. Navajo, Hopi, and Zuni silver and turquoise pieces form the core of the jewelry collection. A number of the early Navajo jewelry examples came from the collection of early trader John Wetherill. 1013 E. University Blvd. at Park Ave. Excluding state holidays, the galleries are open Mon.–Sat. 10 A.M.–5 P.M., Sun. noon–5 P.M. Admission $3 per person. (520) 621-6302 or www.statemuseum.arizona.edu

ASARCO Mineral Discovery Center Located adjacent to the huge ASARCO copper mine complex in Sahuarita, Arizona, south of Tucson, the Mineral Discovery Center provides a fascinating introduction to the process of mining copper, and features a turquoise exhibit as well. Mine tours are available. 1421 W. Pima Mine Road. Open Tues.–Sat., 9 A.M.–5 P.M. Free admission. (520) 625-7513 or www.mineraldiscovery.com

Heard Museum Jewelry collector and turquoise expert C.G. Wallace donated his extensive collection of Southwestern turquoise to this major museum in Phoenix, Arizona. It contains fine examples of Zuni and Navajo turquoise jewelry. 2301 N. Central Ave. at McDowell Road. Open daily 9:30 A.M.–5 P.M. Admission: adults $7, seniors (65+) $6, children (4-12) $3, children under 4 free, Native Americans free. (602) 252-8848 or www.heard.org

Maxwell Museum of Anthropology Located on the campus of the University of New Mexico in Albuquerque, east of University Blvd. between Las Lomas and Dr. M. L. King Jr. Ave., the museum is home to the Shabik'eshchee anthropological collection. Open to the public Tues.–Fri., 9 A.M.–4 P.M.; Sat. 10 A.M.–4 P.M. Closed Sun., Mon., and major holidays. Free admission. (505) 277-4405 or www.maxwell@unm.edu/~maxwell

Queen Mine Tour, Mining & Historical Museum Guided tours of the Queen Mine, located in Bisbee, Arizona, are offered daily at 10:30 A.M., noon, 2 P.M., and 3:30 P.M. Tours leave from the Queen Mine Building. The museum address is 5 Copper Queen Plaza. Open daily 10 A.M.–4 P.M. Bisbee is about ninety miles southeast of Tucson via State Hwy 80. Call (866) 432-2071 for mine tour reservations.

Number 8 turquoise and silver bracelet (courtesy Patania's Sterling Silver Originals)

Millicent Rogers Museum of Northern New Mexico Established in 1956 to display its namesake's outstanding collections of Southwestern arts and crafts, including more than 1,200 pieces of Navajo, Pueblo, and Hispanic jewelry. Located four miles north of Taos, New Mexico, on Millicent Rogers Rd. Open daily 10 A.M.–5 P.M. Closed Mon., November through March, as well as Easter, San Geronimo Day (September 30), Thanksgiving, Christmas, and New Year's Day. Admission: $6 adults, $5 seniors, students and group tours (per person), New Mexico residents $4 (with ID), $12 families, $2 children. Free admission Sun. for Taos County residents (with ID). Members receive a special discount at the Museum Store. (505) 758-2462 or www.millicentrogers.com

Museum of Northern Arizona The museum, located in Flagstaff, Arizona, has major ethnographic collections that contain significant holdings of Hopi and Navajo jewelry. The Hopi Kiva Room and Jewelry Gallery offer additional insight into the daily lives of the people and a chance to see the magnificent artwork they create. Prehistoric collections focus on Ancestral Pueblo cultures and artifacts from various Colorado Plateau archaeological sites. 3101 N. Fort Valley Road. Open 9 A.M.–5 P.M. daily Apr.–Sept., Wed.–Sun. Oct.–Mar., except Thanksgiving, Christmas, and New Year's Day. Admission: $5 adults, $4 seniors, $3 students (18 and older with ID), $2 children. (928) 774-5213 or www.musaz.org

Tucson Gem and Mineral Show Held annually in early February in Tucson, Arizona, this show draws dealers and buyers from around the world and always features a great selection of turquoise and turquoise jewelry. Contact the American Gem Trade Association, (800) 972-1162 or www.tucsonshowguide.com/tsg

Turquoise Museum The Turquoise Museum, located across from Old Town in Albuquerque, New Mexico, houses the largest private collection of turquoise and is one of the world's richest repositories of turquoise mining history, geology, mythology, and folklore. Opened in 1993, the museum celebrates the lifelong labor of J.C. "Zack" and Lillian Zachary. The collection room displays examples of raw and refined turquoise stones and jewelry from more than sixty mines, including all of the "classic mines" in the Southwest. The museum also features a lapidary shop, which demonstrates how turquoise is cut and polished, and offers working demonstrations by Native American silversmiths. Visitors can learn what to look for when buying turquoise jewelry, and in particular Southwestern Indian jewelry, and determine the origin and value of turquoise jewelry they already own. 2107 Central Ave. NW at Rio Grande Blvd. Open Mon.–Sat., 10 A.M.–5 P.M., except New Year's Day, Thanksgiving, and Christmas. (505) 247-8650.

RECOMMENDED READING

Bennett, Edna Mae, and John F. *Turquoise Jewelry of the Indians of the Southwest.* Colorado Springs, Colo.: Turquoise Books, 1973.

Branson, Oscar T. *Turquoise: The Gem of the Centuries.* Tucson, Ariz.: Treasure Chest Publications, Inc., 1976.

Broman, M.G. *Blue Gold: The Turquoise Story.* Anaheim, Calif.: Main Street Press, 1974.

Frazier, Gloria. *Navajos Call It Hard Goods.* Tombstone, Ariz.: Tombstone Printers, 1976.

Hammons, Lee. *Southwestern Turquoise: The Indian Sky Stone* (2nd ed.). Glendale, Ariz.: Arizona Maps & Books, 1976.

Hammons, Lee, and Gertrude Frances Hill. *Turquoise and the Navajo.* Glendale, AZ: Arizona Maps & Books, 1975.

Hodge, Frederick Webb. *Turquois Work of Hawikuh, New Mexico.* New York: Museum of the American Indian, 1921.

Hodge, Frederick Webb, and Jesse Walter Fewkes. *Decoration Designs: Turquoise and Pottery.* Albuquerque, NM: Calvin Horn Publisher, Inc., 1974.

Jacka, Jerry D., and Spencer Gill. *Turquoise Treasures: The Splendor of Southwest Indian Art.* Portland, Ore.: Graphic Arts Center Pub. Co., 1975.

Judd, N.M. *The Material Culture of Pueblo Bonito.* Smithsonian Miscellaneous Collections No. 124. Washington, DC: Smithsonian Institution, 1954.

Karasik, Carol. *The Turquoise Trail: Native American Jewelry and Culture of the Southwest.* New York: Harry Abrams, 1993.

Pogue, Joseph E. *Turquois: A Study of Its History, Mineralogy, Geology, Ethnology, Archaeology, Mythology, Folklore, andTechnology.* Washington, DC: National Academy of Sciences, 1915. (Reprinted 1972 by Rio Grande Press of Glorieta, NM.)

Stacy, Joseph, ed. *Turquoise Blue Book and Indian Jewelry Digest.* Phoenix, Ariz.: Arizona Highways, 1975.

Tanner, Clara Lee, and Joe Ben Wheat. *Ray Manley's Portraits & Turquoise of Southwest Indians.* Tucson, Ariz.: Ray Manley Photography, 1975.

Vigil, Arnold, ed. *The Allure of Turquoise* by Susan Arritt, et. al. others. Santa Fe: *New Mexico Magazine*, 1995.

Windes, Thomas C. "Blue Notes: The Chacoan Turquoise Industry in the San Juan Basin." In *Anasazi Regional Organization and the Chaco System*, edited by D.E. Doyel. Maxwell Museum of Anthropology Anthropological Papers No. 5. Albuquerque, NM: University of New Mexico, 1992.

Photo Credits

*Number 8 turquoise and coral
necklace (courtesy Patania's
Sterling Silver Originals)*

Index

Blue Gem turquoise and silver box (courtesy Patania's Sterling Silver Originals)